£3-50

To ....

From ....

ALiᵉᵃt

Alicat Trading Pty Ltd
140 Albert Road
South Melbourne VIC 3205
Australia
Email: publishing@alicat.com.au

Publisher Ali Horgan
Design Canary Graphic Design
Production Angie McKenzie

First published 2010

Printed in China 5 4 3 2 1

INSPIRATIONAL QUOTATIONS

FEELINGS
from the HEART

Life is short
and we have never too much time
for gladdening the hearts
of those who are travelling
the dark journey with us.
Oh, be swift to love,
make haste to be kind.

Henri–Frederic Amiel

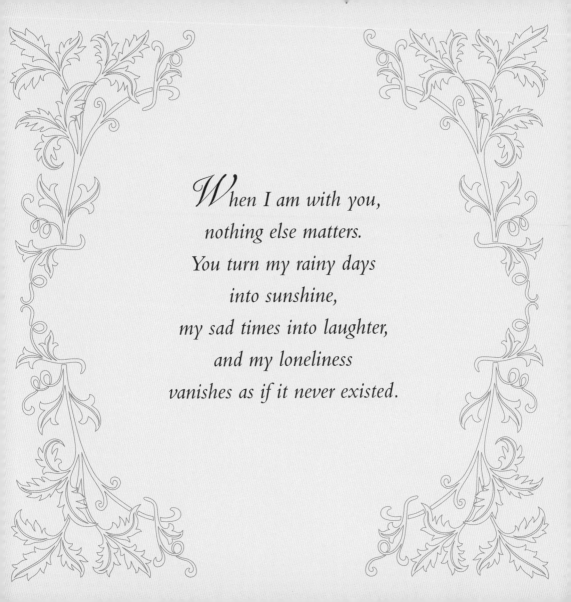

When I am with you,
nothing else matters.
You turn my rainy days
into sunshine,
my sad times into laughter,
and my loneliness
vanishes as if it never existed.

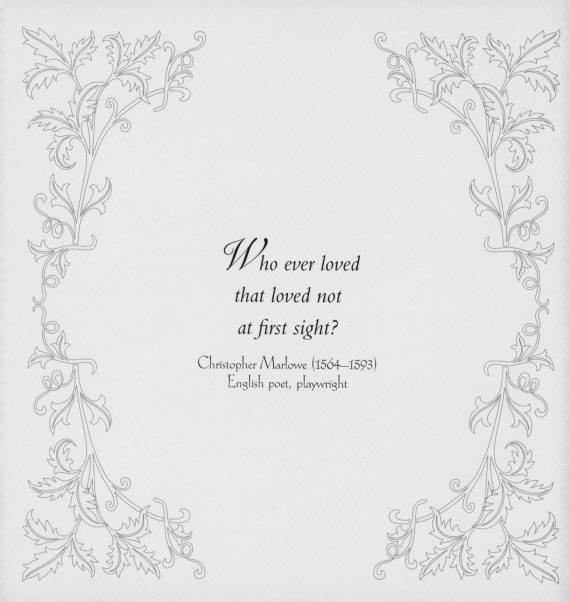

Who ever loved
that loved not
at first sight?

Christopher Marlowe (1564–1593)
English poet, playwright

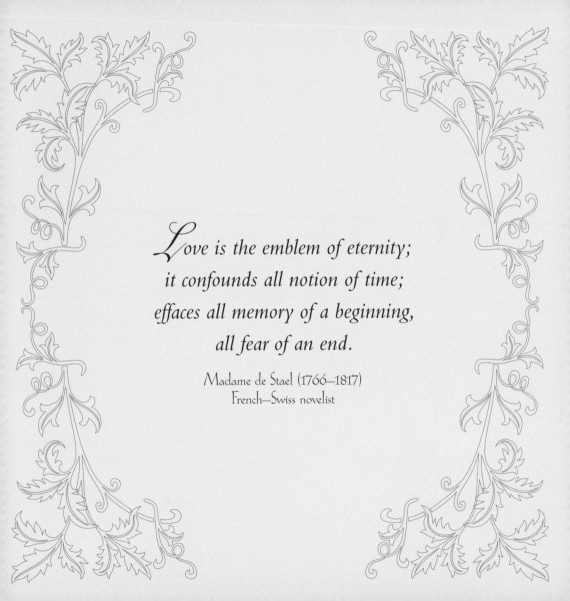

Love is the emblem of eternity;
it confounds all notion of time;
effaces all memory of a beginning,
all fear of an end.

Madame de Stael (1766–1817)
French–Swiss novelist

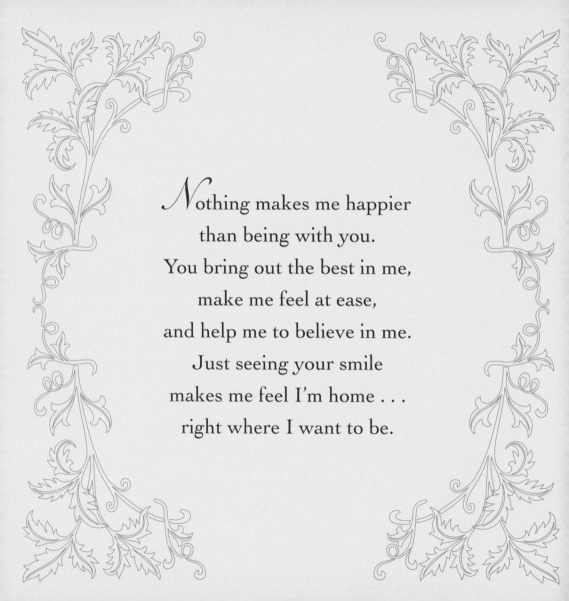

*N*othing makes me happier
than being with you.
You bring out the best in me,
make me feel at ease,
and help me to believe in me.
Just seeing your smile
makes me feel I'm home . . .
right where I want to be.

First romance,
first love,
is something so special to all of us,
both emotionally and physically,
that it touches our lives and enriches
them forever.

Rosemary Rogers

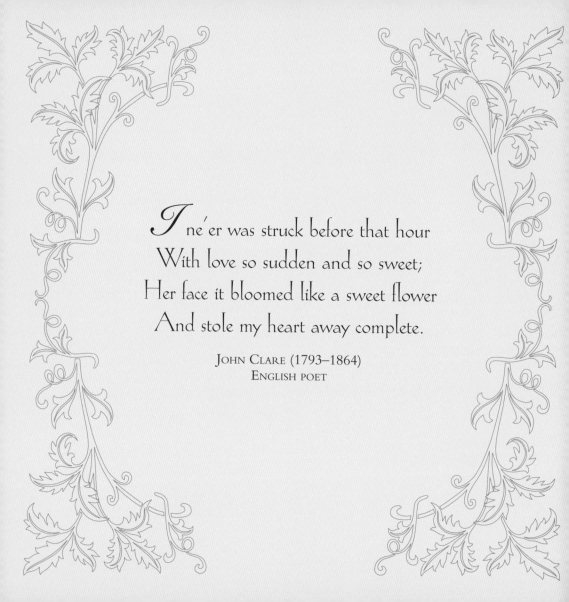

I ne'er was struck before that hour
With love so sudden and so sweet;
Her face it bloomed like a sweet flower
And stole my heart away complete.

JOHN CLARE (1793–1864)
ENGLISH POET

$\mathcal{F}$irst love is a little foolish
and a lot of curiosity.

GEORGE BERNARD SHAW

But to see her
was to love her,
love but her,
and love forever.

Robert Burns (1759–1796)
Scottish poet

$\mathcal{W}$e never forget those
that make us blush.

JEAN–FRANÇOIS DE LA HARPE

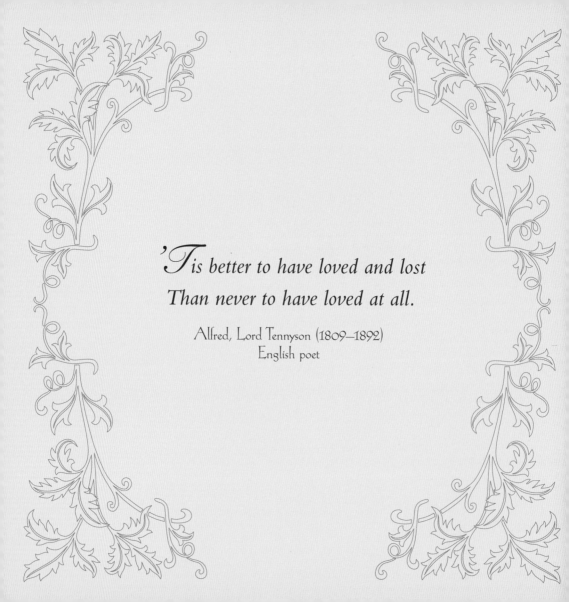

'*T*is better to have loved and lost
Than never to have loved at all.

Alfred, Lord Tennyson (1809–1892)
English poet

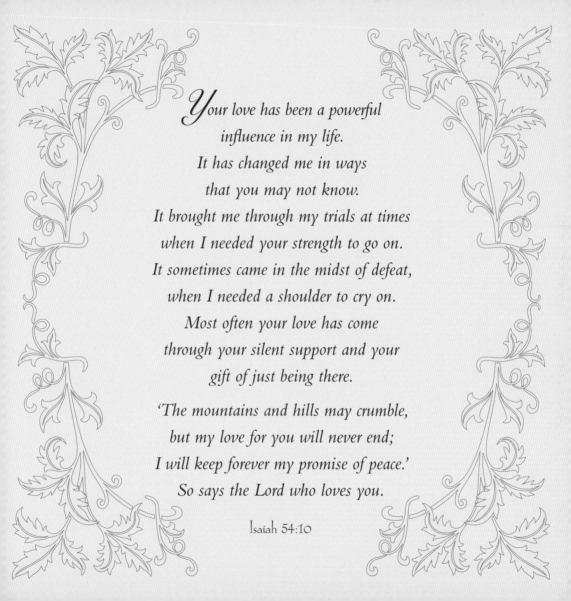

Your love has been a powerful
influence in my life.
It has changed me in ways
that you may not know.
It brought me through my trials at times
when I needed your strength to go on.
It sometimes came in the midst of defeat,
when I needed a shoulder to cry on.
Most often your love has come
through your silent support and your
gift of just being there.

'The mountains and hills may crumble,
but my love for you will never end;
I will keep forever my promise of peace.'
So says the Lord who loves you.

Isaiah 54:10

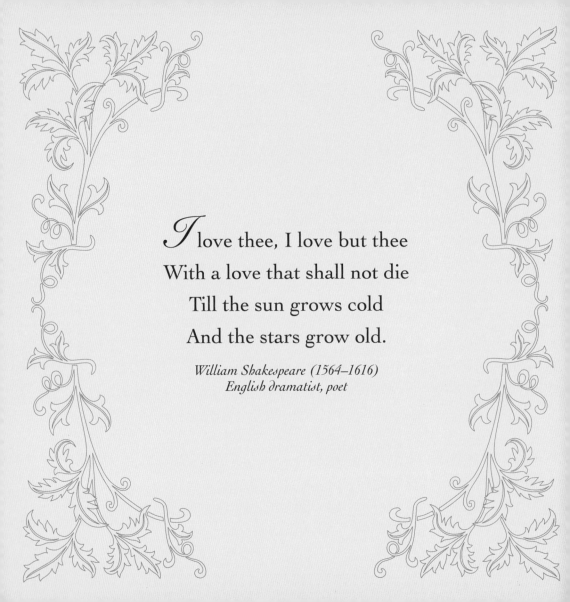

I love thee, I love but thee
With a love that shall not die
Till the sun grows cold
And the stars grow old.

William Shakespeare (1564–1616)
English dramatist, poet

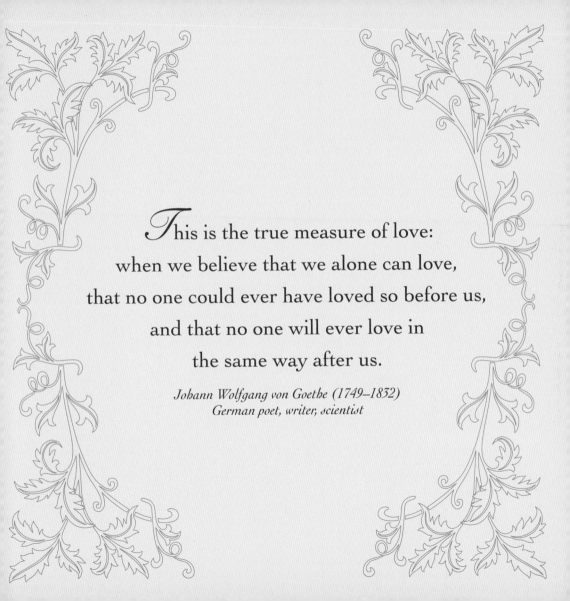

This is the true measure of love:
when we believe that we alone can love,
that no one could ever have loved so before us,
and that no one will ever love in
the same way after us.

Johann Wolfgang von Goethe (1749–1832)
German poet, writer, scientist

*Love is an act
of endless forgiveness,
a tender look
which becomes a habit.*

Peter Ustinov (1921–2004)
British actor, director, writer

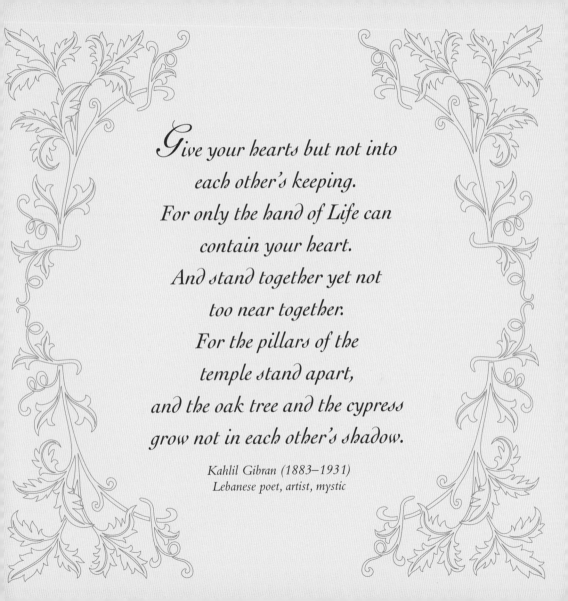

Give your hearts but not into
each other's keeping.
For only the hand of Life can
contain your heart.
And stand together yet not
too near together.
For the pillars of the
temple stand apart,
and the oak tree and the cypress
grow not in each other's shadow.

Kahlil Gibran (1883–1931)
Lebanese poet, artist, mystic

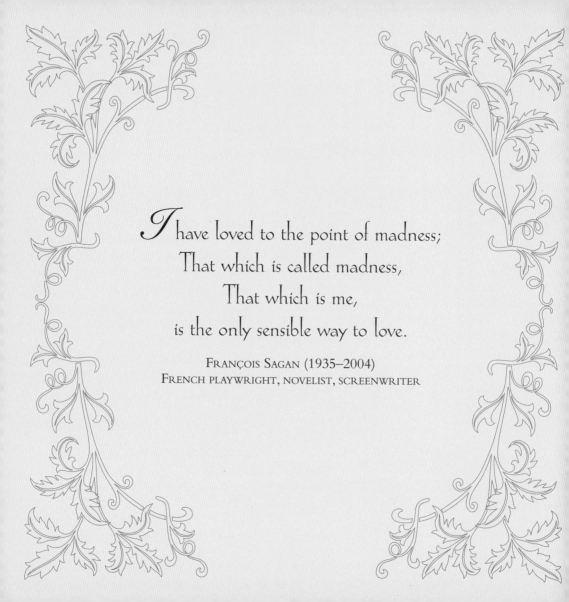

$\mathcal{I}$ have loved to the point of madness;
That which is called madness,
That which is me,
is the only sensible way to love.

FRANÇOIS SAGAN (1935–2004)
FRENCH PLAYWRIGHT, NOVELIST, SCREENWRITER

*L*ove is something eternal; the aspect
may change, but not the essence.

Vincent van Gogh

A light heart lives long.

William Shakespeare (1564–1616)
English dramatist, poet

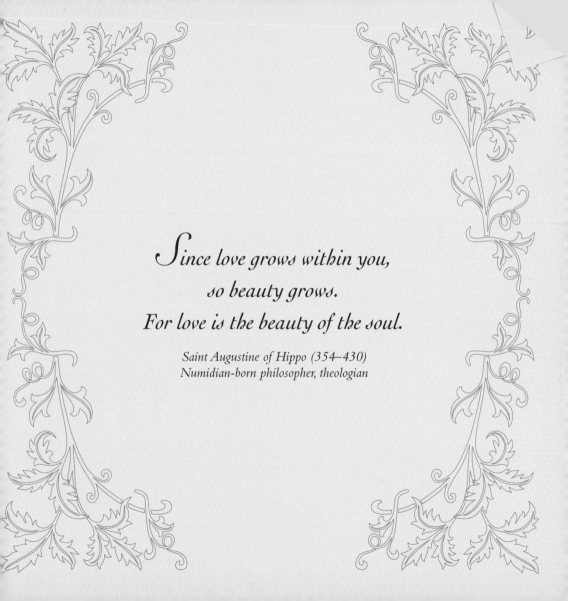

*S*ince love grows within you,

so beauty grows.

For love is the beauty of the soul.

Saint Augustine of Hippo (354–430)
Numidian-born philosopher, theologian

*L*et's say we'll stay together . . .

just we two.

Let's pray whatever comes our way,

we'll make it through.

Let's promise that until the end

we'll both be true.

And with our final breath,

let's whisper,

"I love you."

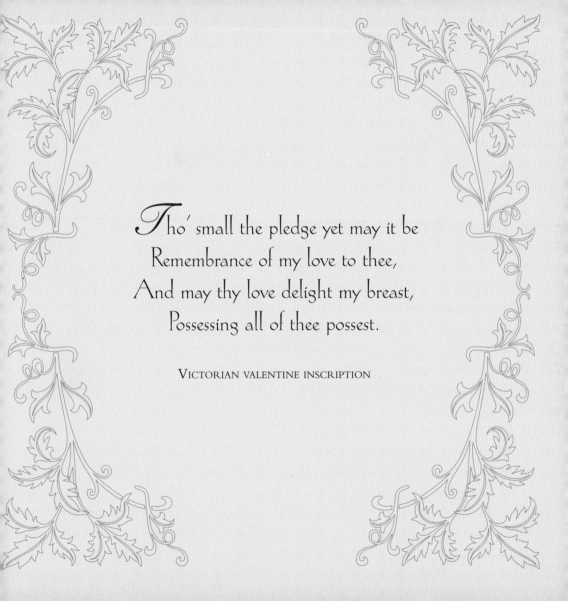

Tho' small the pledge yet may it be
Remembrance of my love to thee,
And may thy love delight my breast,
Possessing all of thee possest.

VICTORIAN VALENTINE INSCRIPTION

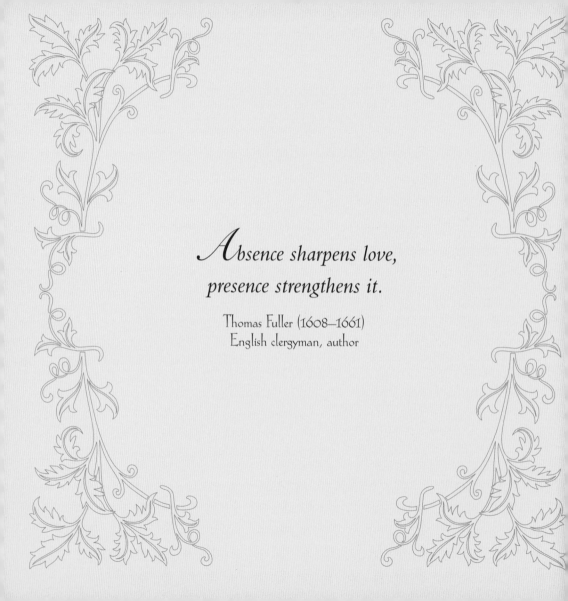

*Absence sharpens love,
presence strengthens it.*

Thomas Fuller (1608–1661)
English clergyman, author

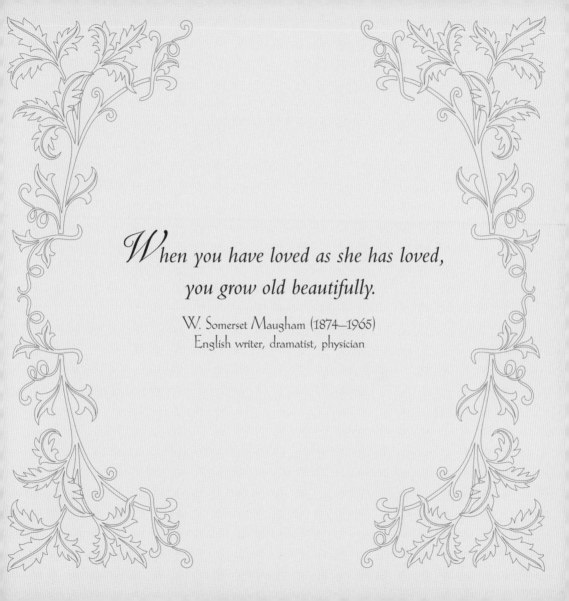

*W*hen you have loved as she has loved,
you grow old beautifully.

W. Somerset Maugham (1874–1965)
English writer, dramatist, physician

*L*ove those that love you.

Voltaire (1694–1778)
French poet

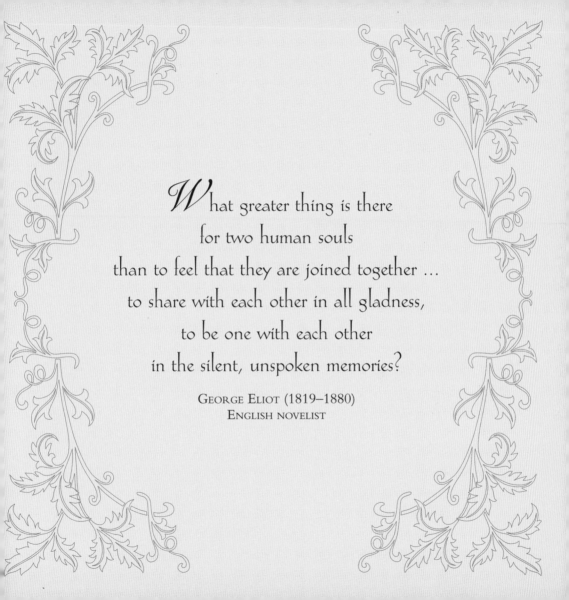

*W*hat greater thing is there
for two human souls
than to feel that they are joined together …
to share with each other in all gladness,
to be one with each other
in the silent, unspoken memories?

GEORGE ELIOT (1819–1880)
ENGLISH NOVELIST

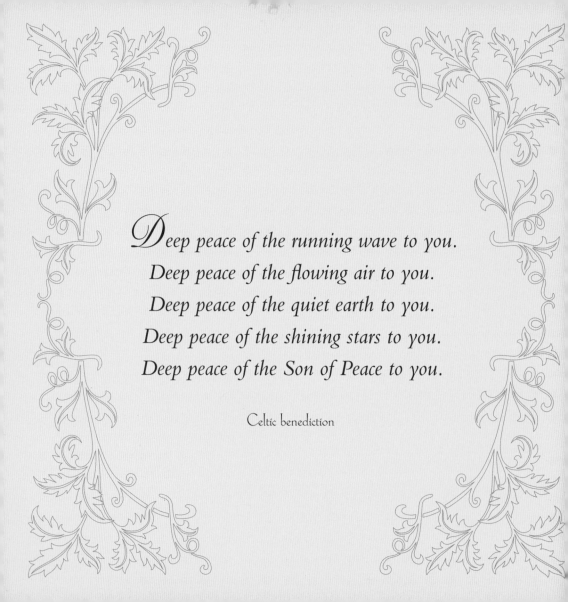

Deep peace of the running wave to you.
Deep peace of the flowing air to you.
Deep peace of the quiet earth to you.
Deep peace of the shining stars to you.
Deep peace of the Son of Peace to you.

Celtic benediction

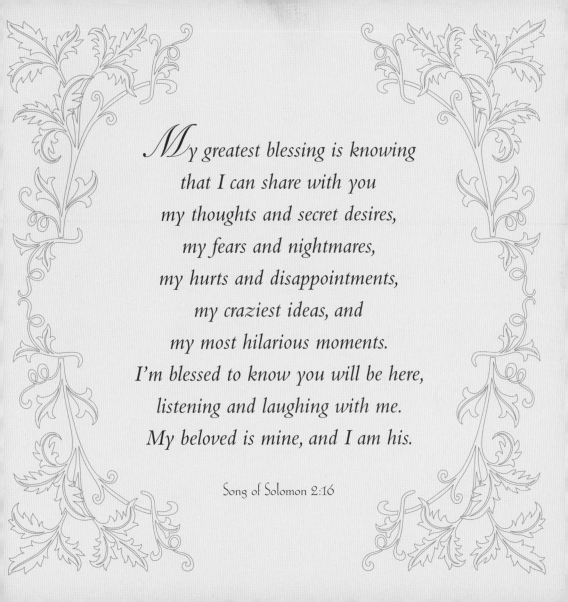

My greatest blessing is knowing
that I can share with you
my thoughts and secret desires,
my fears and nightmares,
my hurts and disappointments,
my craziest ideas, and
my most hilarious moments.
I'm blessed to know you will be here,
listening and laughing with me.
My beloved is mine, and I am his.

Song of Solomon 2:16

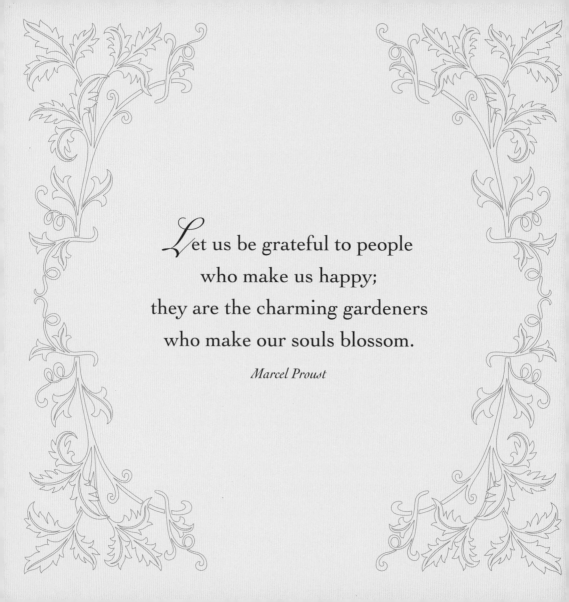

*L*et us be grateful to people
who make us happy;
they are the charming gardeners
who make our souls blossom.

Marcel Proust

*L*ove is like war:
Easy to begin but hard to end.

The most wonderful of all things in life,
I believe, is the discovery of another
human being with whom one's relationship
has a glowing depth, beauty and joy
as the years increase.
This inner progressiveness of love
between two human beings
is a most marvellous thing,
it cannot be found by looking for it
or by passionately wishing for it.
It is a sort of Divine accident.

Sir Hugh Seymour Walpole (1884–1941)
English critic, dramatist

You are always new.
The last of your kisses

was ever the sweetest.

John Keats (1795–1821)
English poet

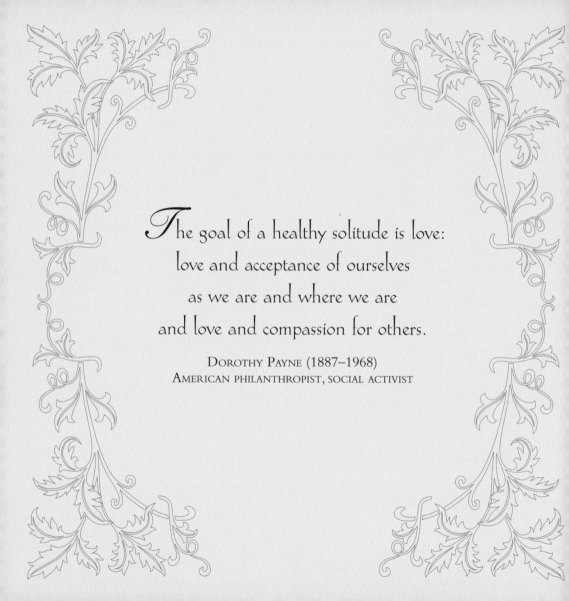

The goal of a healthy solitude is love:
love and acceptance of ourselves
as we are and where we are
and love and compassion for others.

DOROTHY PAYNE (1887–1968)
AMERICAN PHILANTHROPIST, SOCIAL ACTIVIST

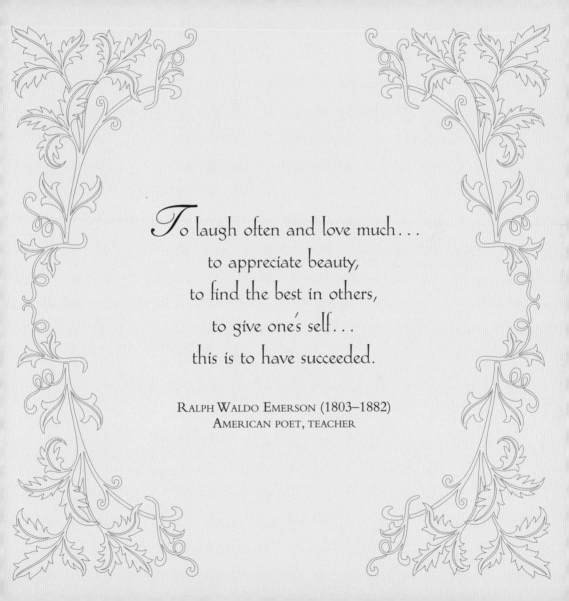

$\mathcal{T}$o laugh often and love much...
to appreciate beauty,
to find the best in others,
to give one's self...
this is to have succeeded.

RALPH WALDO EMERSON (1803–1882)
AMERICAN POET, TEACHER

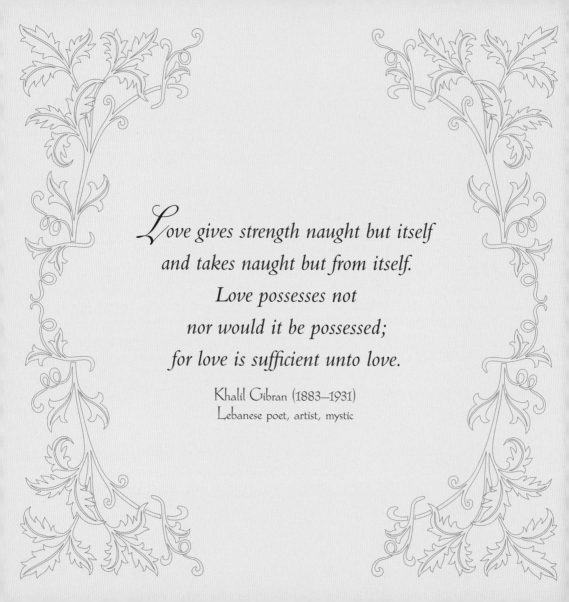

Love gives strength naught but itself
and takes naught but from itself.
Love possesses not
nor would it be possessed;
for love is sufficient unto love.

Khalil Gibran (1883–1931)
Lebanese poet, artist, mystic

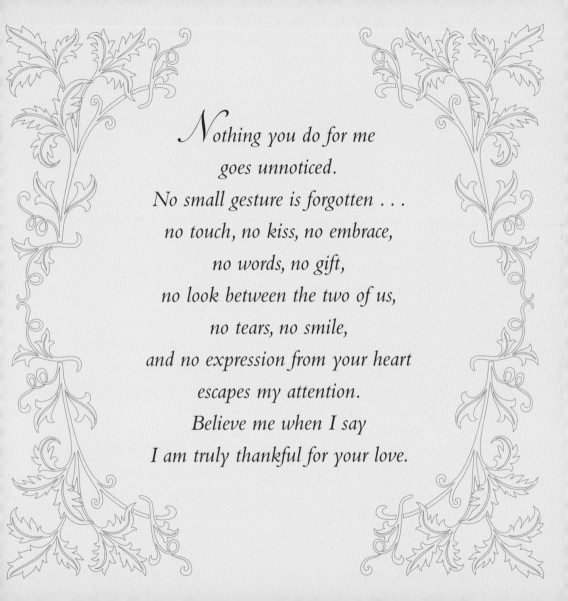

Nothing you do for me
goes unnoticed.
No small gesture is forgotten . . .
no touch, no kiss, no embrace,
no words, no gift,
no look between the two of us,
no tears, no smile,
and no expression from your heart
escapes my attention.
Believe me when I say
I am truly thankful for your love.

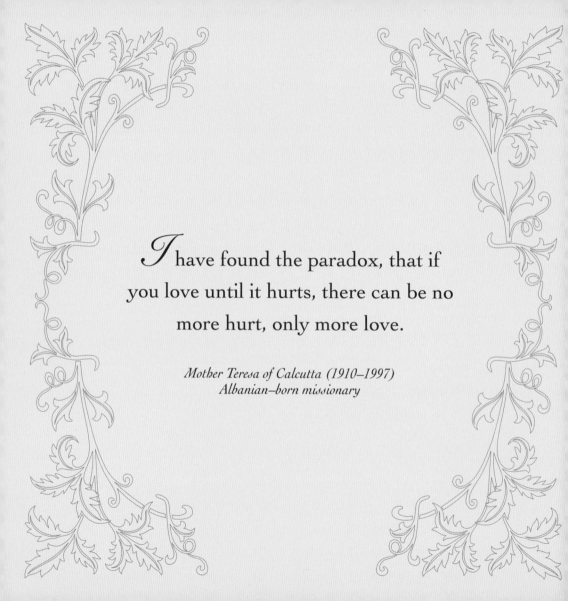

I have found the paradox, that if you love until it hurts, there can be no more hurt, only more love.

Mother Teresa of Calcutta (1910–1997)
Albanian–born missionary

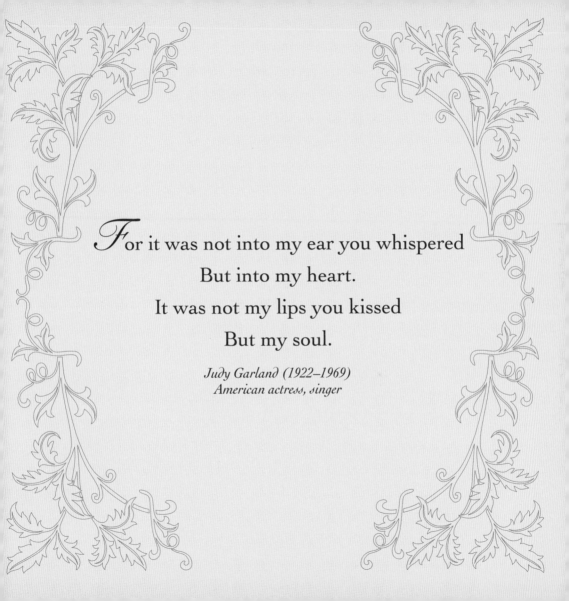

For it was not into my ear you whispered

But into my heart.

It was not my lips you kissed

But my soul.

Judy Garland (1922–1969)
American actress, singer

*The most wasted day
is that in which
we have not laughed.*

Chamfort

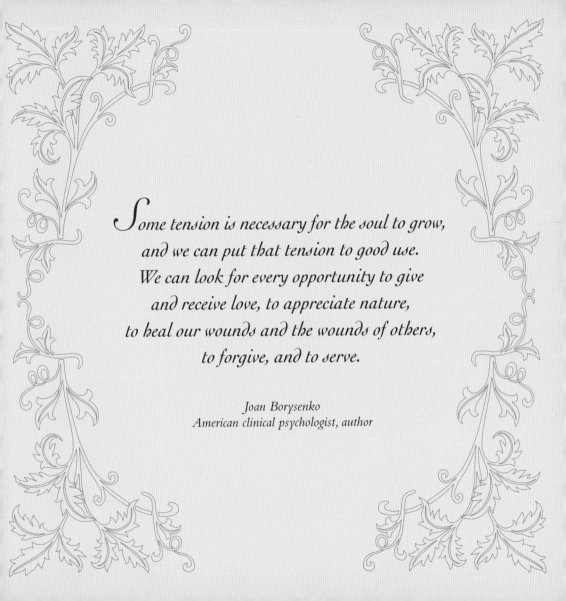

*Some tension is necessary for the soul to grow,
and we can put that tension to good use.
We can look for every opportunity to give
and receive love, to appreciate nature,
to heal our wounds and the wounds of others,
to forgive, and to serve.*

Joan Borysenko
American clinical psychologist, author

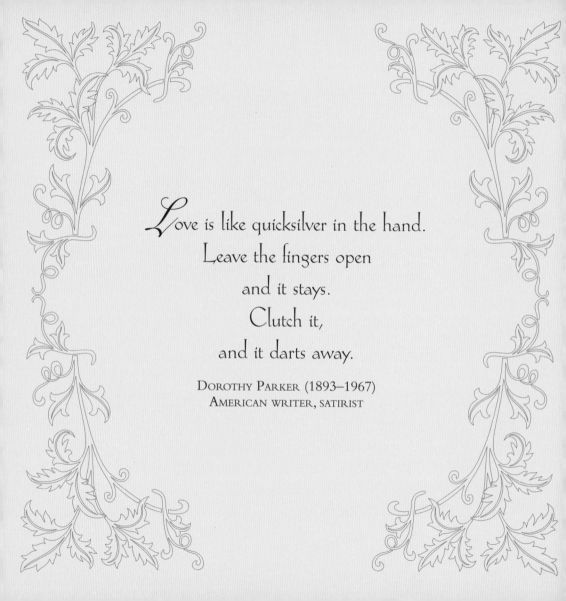

*L*ove is like quicksilver in the hand.
Leave the fingers open
and it stays.
Clutch it,
and it darts away.

DOROTHY PARKER (1893–1967)
AMERICAN WRITER, SATIRIST

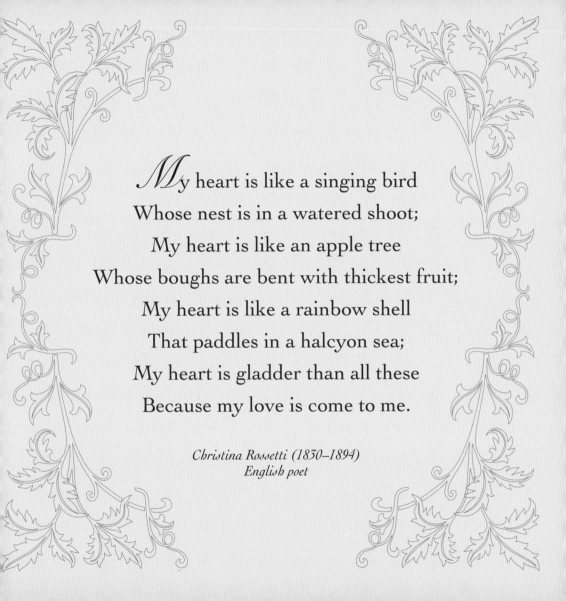

My heart is like a singing bird
Whose nest is in a watered shoot;
My heart is like an apple tree
Whose boughs are bent with thickest fruit;
My heart is like a rainbow shell
That paddles in a halcyon sea;
My heart is gladder than all these
Because my love is come to me.

Christina Rossetti (1830–1894)
English poet

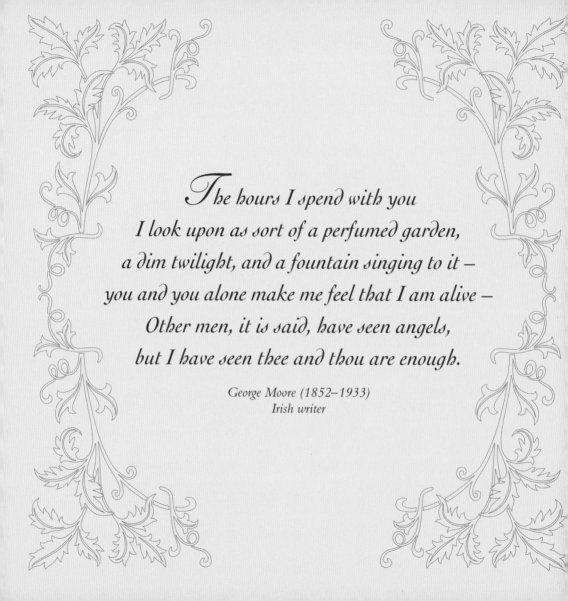

The hours I spend with you
I look upon as sort of a perfumed garden,
a dim twilight, and a fountain singing to it —
you and you alone make me feel that I am alive —
Other men, it is said, have seen angels,
but I have seen thee and thou are enough.

George Moore (1852–1933)
Irish writer

To love is to receive a glimpse of heaven.

Karen Sunde

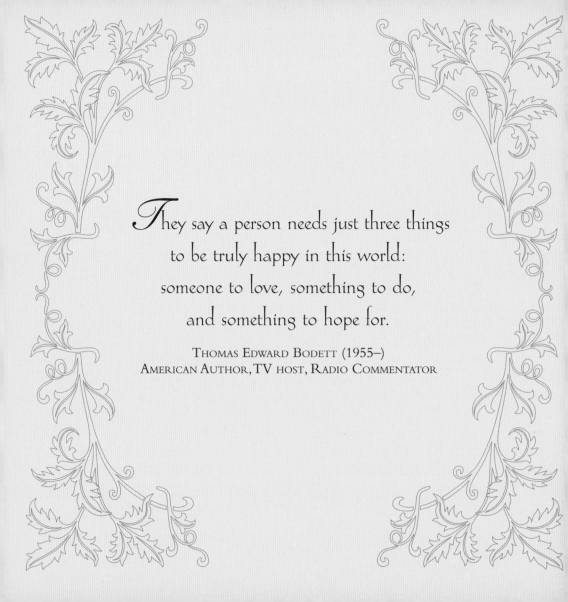

They say a person needs just three things
to be truly happy in this world:
someone to love, something to do,
and something to hope for.

THOMAS EDWARD BODETT (1955–)
AMERICAN AUTHOR, TV HOST, RADIO COMMENTATOR

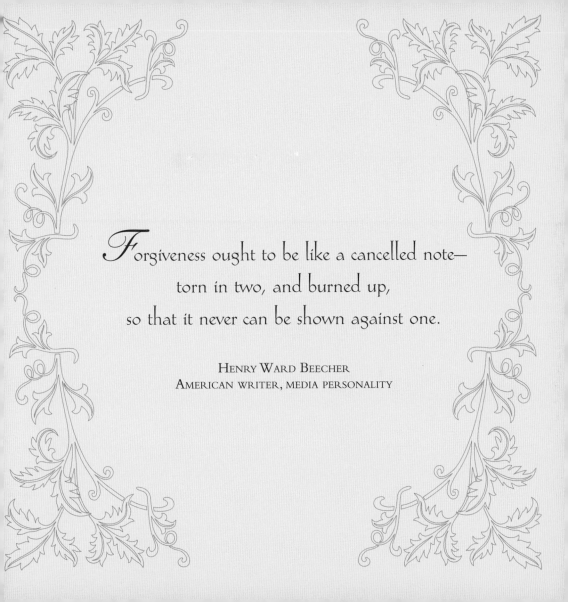

Forgiveness ought to be like a cancelled note—
torn in two, and burned up,
so that it never can be shown against one.

HENRY WARD BEECHER
AMERICAN WRITER, MEDIA PERSONALITY

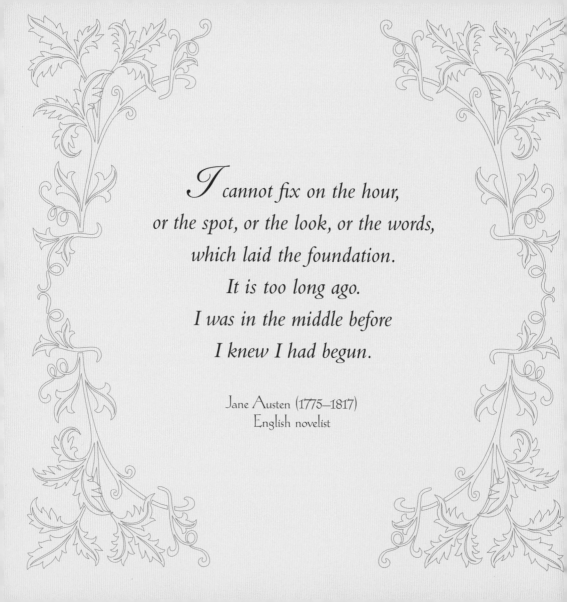

*I cannot fix on the hour,
or the spot, or the look, or the words,
which laid the foundation.
It is too long ago.
I was in the middle before
I knew I had begun.*

Jane Austen (1775–1817)
English novelist

Nobody has ever measured,
not even poets,
how much the heart can hold.

Zelda Fitzgerald (1900–1948)
American writer

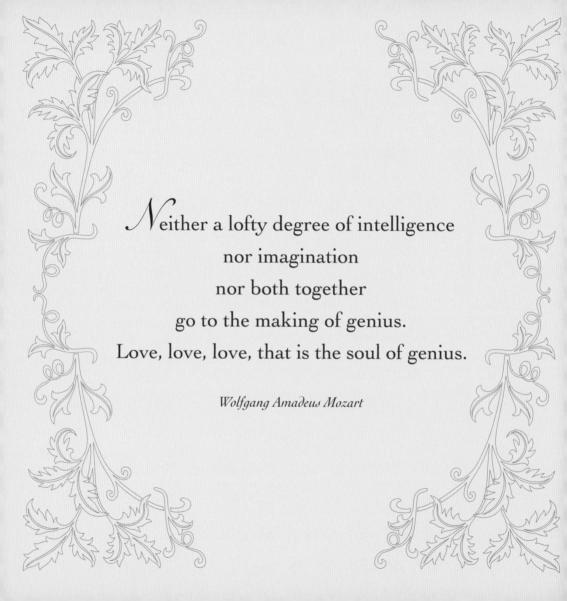

*N*either a lofty degree of intelligence
nor imagination
nor both together
go to the making of genius.
Love, love, love, that is the soul of genius.

Wolfgang Amadeus Mozart

It is not night when I do see your face.

WILLIAM SHAKESPEARE (1564–1616)
ENGLISH DRAMATIST, POET

Whatever our souls are made of,
his and mine are the same.

Emily Brontë
English novelist, poet

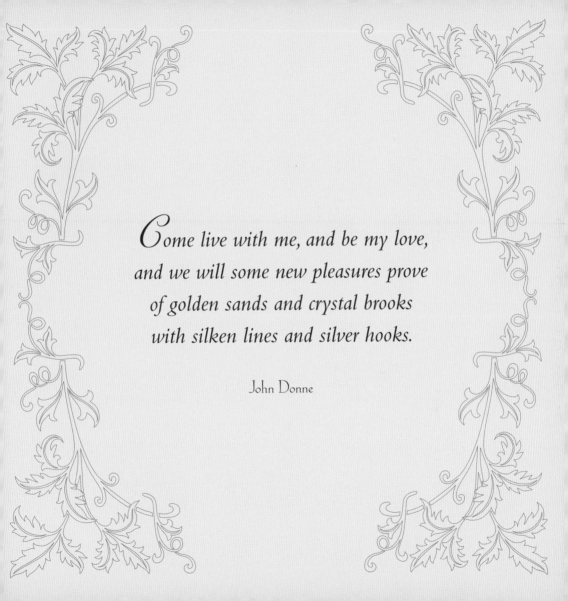

Come live with me, and be my love,
and we will some new pleasures prove
of golden sands and crystal brooks
with silken lines and silver hooks.

John Donne

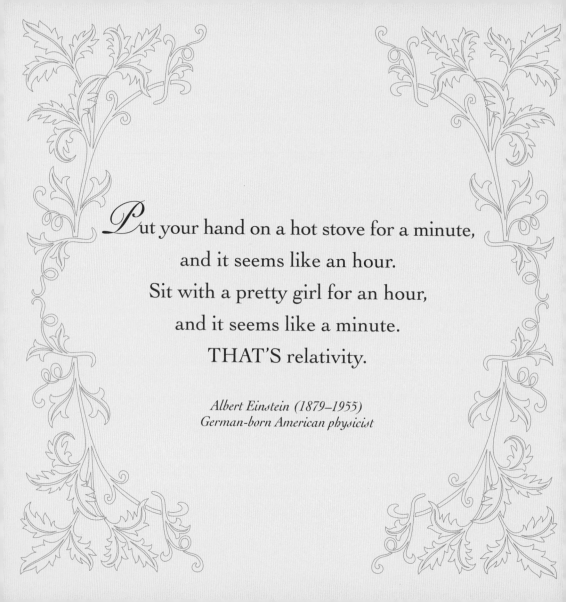

*P*ut your hand on a hot stove for a minute,
and it seems like an hour.
Sit with a pretty girl for an hour,
and it seems like a minute.
THAT'S relativity.

Albert Einstein (1879–1955)
German-born American physicist

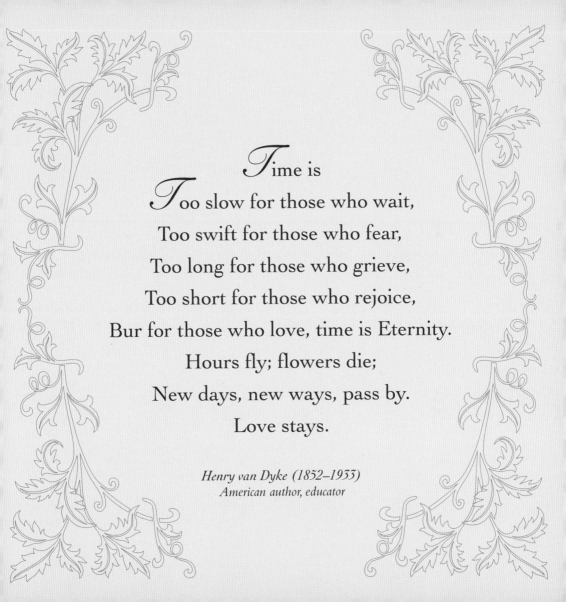

*T*ime is
*T*oo slow for those who wait,
Too swift for those who fear,
Too long for those who grieve,
Too short for those who rejoice,
Bur for those who love, time is Eternity.
Hours fly; flowers die;
New days, new ways, pass by.
Love stays.

Henry van Dyke (1852–1933)
American author, educator

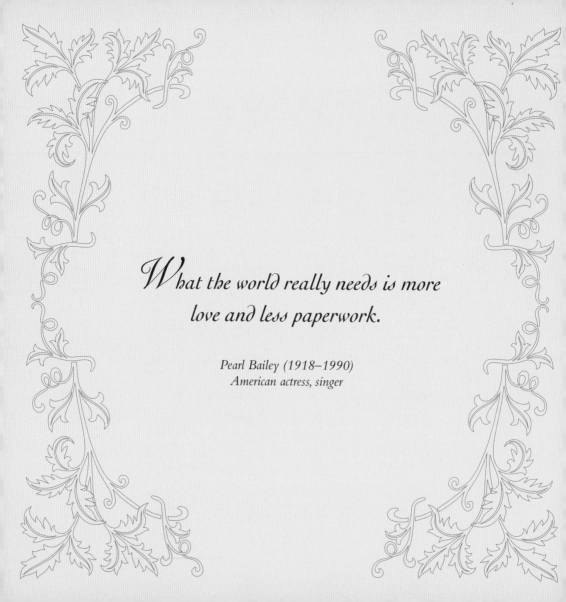

*What the world really needs is more
love and less paperwork.*

Pearl Bailey (1918–1990)
American actress, singer

At first I thought we were just friends:
fun talks, short walks, coffee breaks
that never seemed to end.
And then you kissed me.
You simply caught me off guard
and placed a soft and tender kiss
on the back of my neck.
It was at that very moment,
I knew we were no longer just friends.
I ran up the stairs, opened the door,
put on my pyjamas — and said my prayers,
turned off my light, tumbled into my bed,
and all because he kissed me good-night!

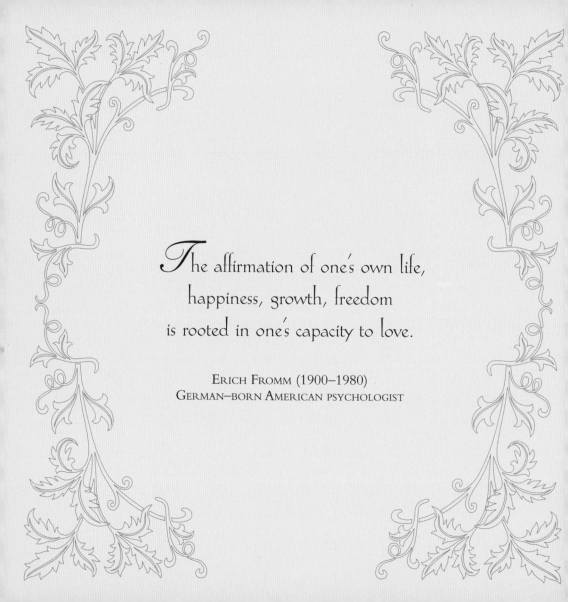

The affirmation of one's own life,
happiness, growth, freedom
is rooted in one's capacity to love.

ERICH FROMM (1900–1980)
GERMAN–BORN AMERICAN PSYCHOLOGIST

*W*hat is a friend?
A single soul
dwelling in two bodies.

ARISTOTLE

Let's be friends forever.
Let's defend, protect, and build
on what we have.
Let's love for love's sake
and continue to overlook mistakes.
Let's dream and reach higher
and be stubborn in our
determination to see the other succeed.
Let's be friends forever.

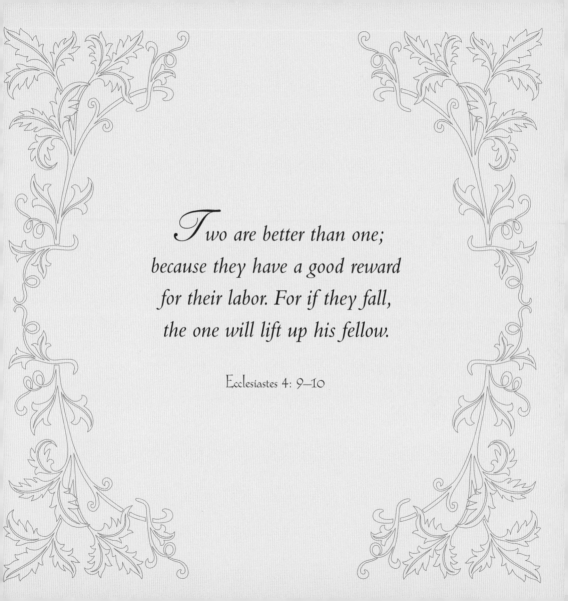

*Two are better than one;
because they have a good reward
for their labor. For if they fall,
the one will lift up his fellow.*

Ecclesiastes 4: 9–10

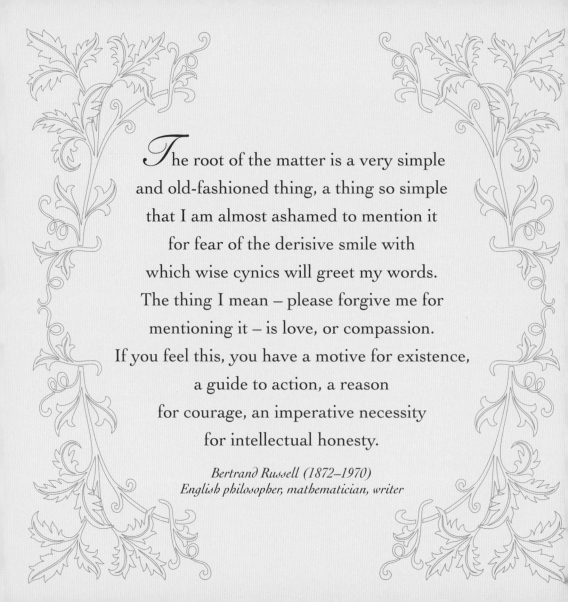

The root of the matter is a very simple
and old-fashioned thing, a thing so simple
that I am almost ashamed to mention it
for fear of the derisive smile with
which wise cynics will greet my words.
The thing I mean – please forgive me for
mentioning it – is love, or compassion.
If you feel this, you have a motive for existence,
a guide to action, a reason
for courage, an imperative necessity
for intellectual honesty.

Bertrand Russell (1872–1970)
English philosopher, mathematician, writer

If, from time to time,
we look at the blessings in our lives,
at the warmth and care and love
so many people respond with when
there is a tragedy,
at the fact that we can walk and talk
and eat and breathe, then maybe we would…
become aware that all negative thoughts
bring with them are more negativity,
but love shared returns a thousandfold.

Elisabeth Kubler–Ross (1926–2004)
Swiss–born American psychiatrist

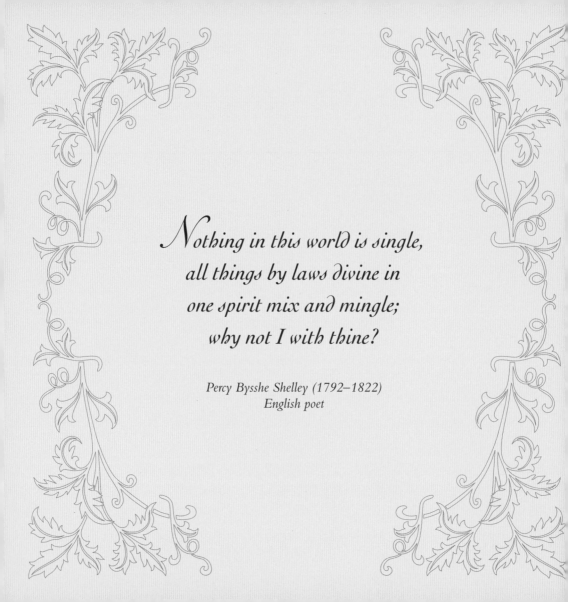

Nothing in this world is single,
all things by laws divine in
one spirit mix and mingle;
why not I with thine?

Percy Bysshe Shelley (1792–1822)
English poet

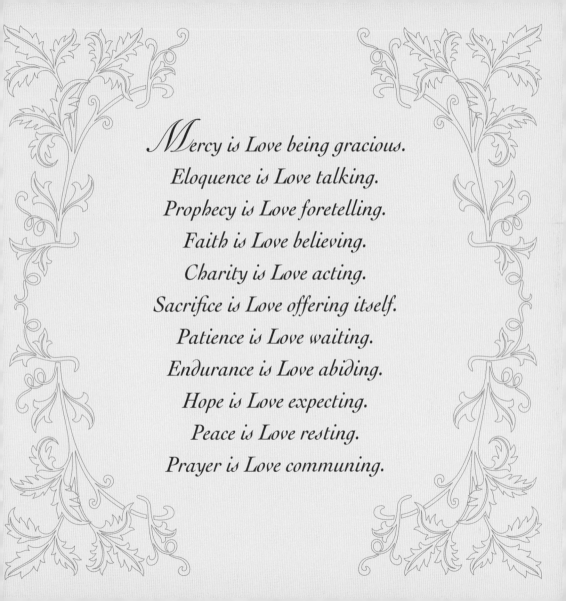

Mercy is Love being gracious.
Eloquence is Love talking.
Prophecy is Love foretelling.
Faith is Love believing.
Charity is Love acting.
Sacrifice is Love offering itself.
Patience is Love waiting.
Endurance is Love abiding.
Hope is Love expecting.
Peace is Love resting.
Prayer is Love communing.

I tried with all my heart
to hide the fact that
I was falling in love.
I was giddy, losing weight,
and doing all of the obvious things
people do when they fall in love.
Yet I still tried to hide it.
Then one day,
out came the words like water
from a fountain, and my secret
was exposed to the world.
I love you!

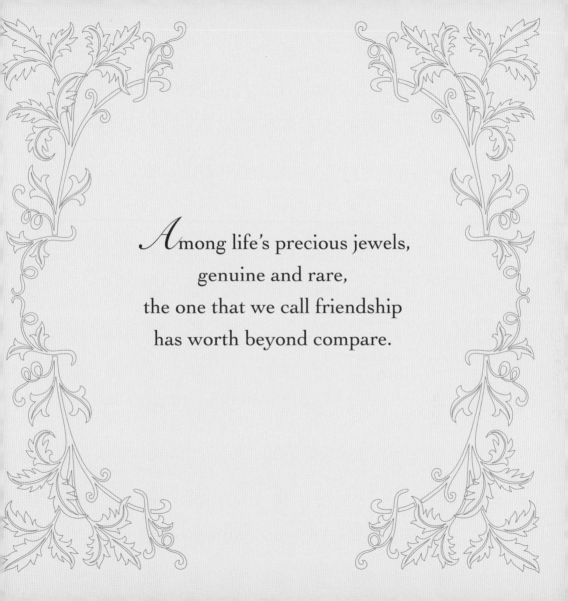

*A*mong life's precious jewels,

genuine and rare,

the one that we call friendship

has worth beyond compare.

For where your treasure is, there your heart will be also.

Luke 12:34

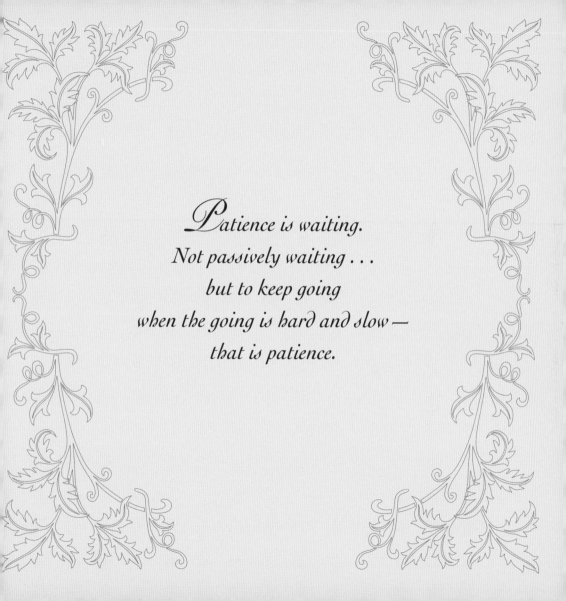

Patience is waiting.
Not passively waiting . . .
but to keep going
when the going is hard and slow —
that is patience.

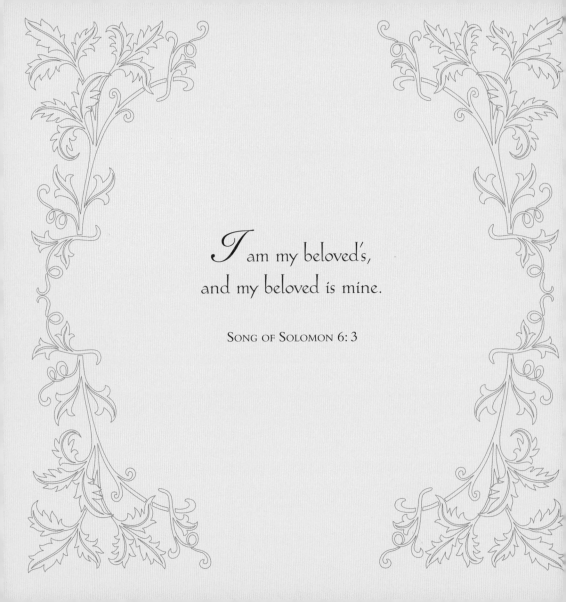

I am my beloved's,
and my beloved is mine.

SONG OF SOLOMON 6: 3

You are my love, my best friend,
my life, and my heart and soul.
You move me to be a better person.

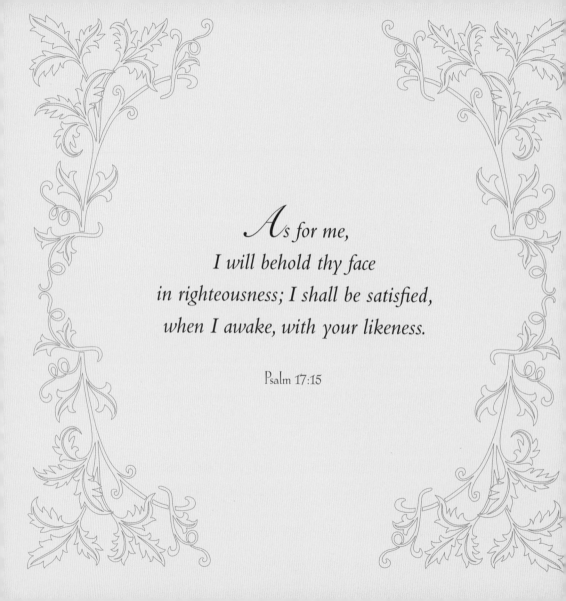

As for me,
I will behold thy face
in righteousness; I shall be satisfied,
when I awake, with your likeness.

Psalm 17:15

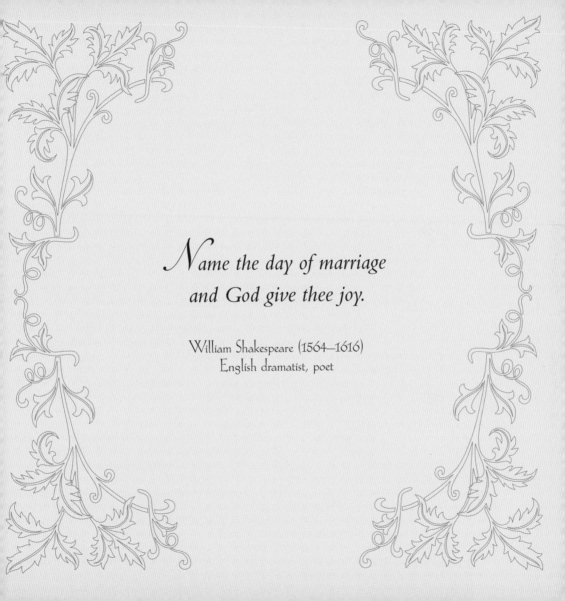

Name the day of marriage
and God give thee joy.

William Shakespeare (1564–1616)
English dramatist, poet

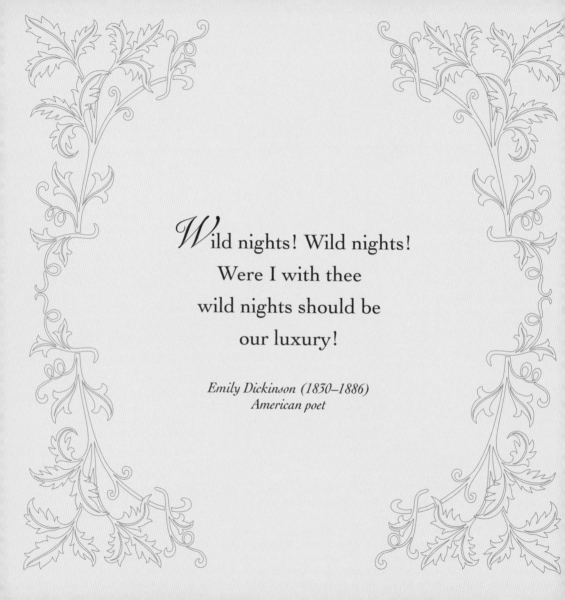

*W*ild nights! Wild nights!
Were I with thee
wild nights should be
our luxury!

Emily Dickinson (1830–1886)
American poet

*R*evere.

Cherish.

Honour.

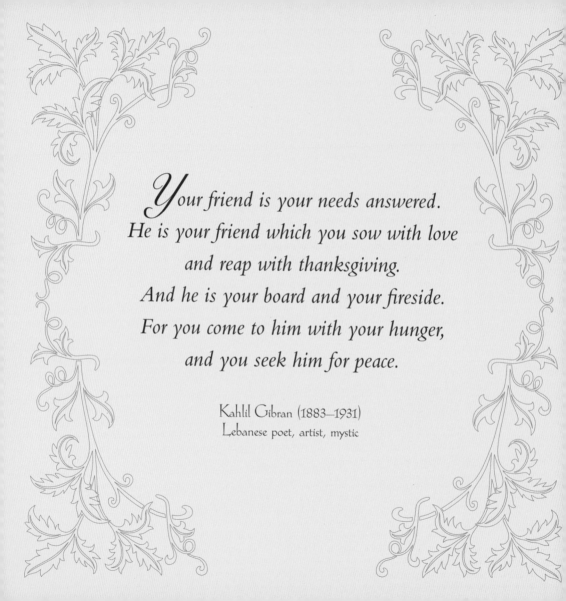

Your friend is your needs answered.
He is your friend which you sow with love
and reap with thanksgiving.
And he is your board and your fireside.
For you come to him with your hunger,
and you seek him for peace.

Kahlil Gibran (1883–1931)
Lebanese poet, artist, mystic

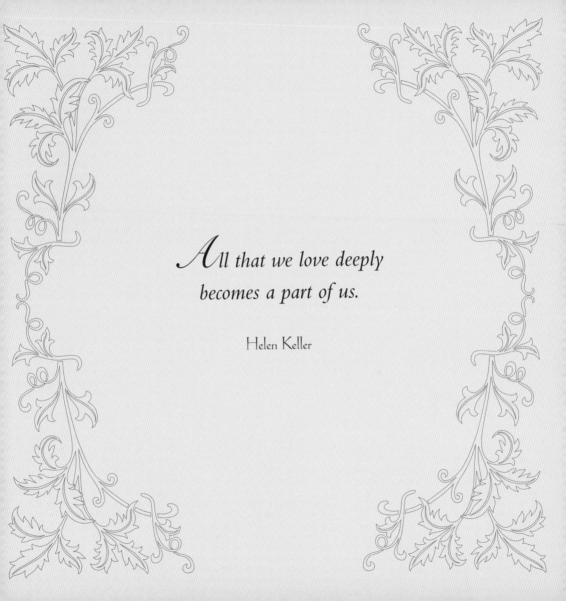

*A*ll that we love deeply
becomes a part of us.

Helen Keller

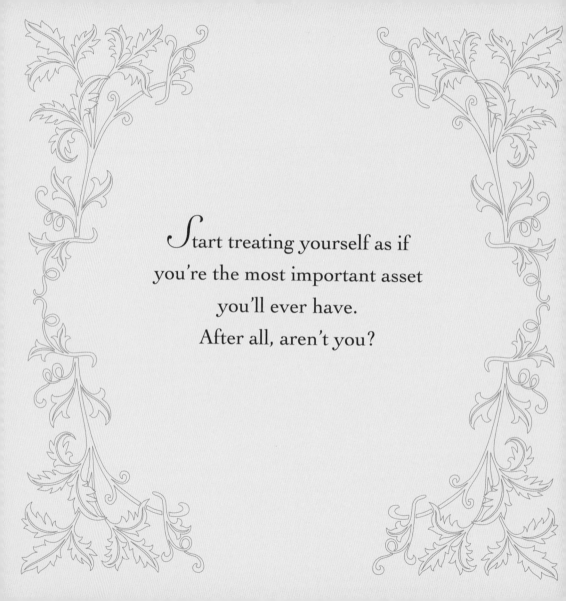

$\int$tart treating yourself as if
you're the most important asset
you'll ever have.
After all, aren't you?

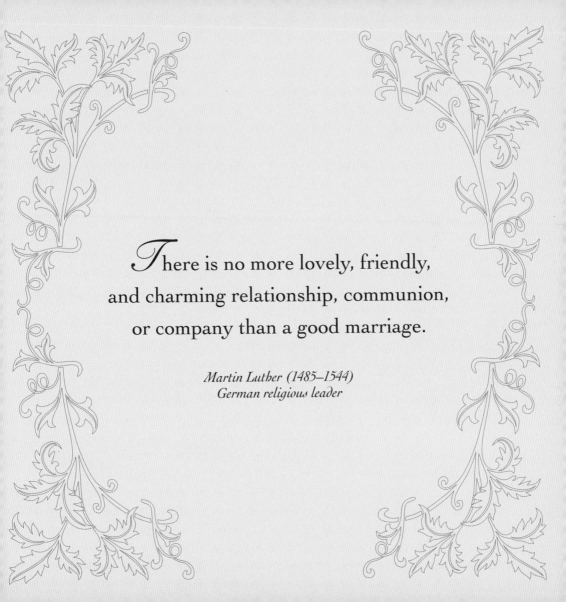

There is no more lovely, friendly,
and charming relationship, communion,
or company than a good marriage.

Martin Luther (1485–1544)
German religious leader

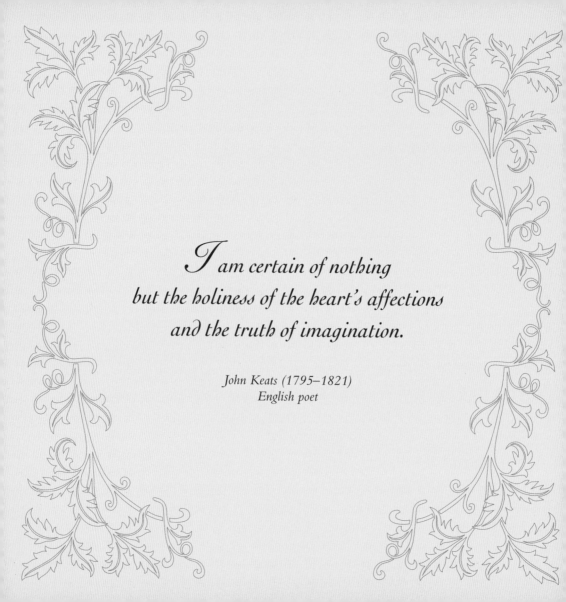

*I am certain of nothing
but the holiness of the heart's affections
and the truth of imagination.*

John Keats (1795–1821)
English poet

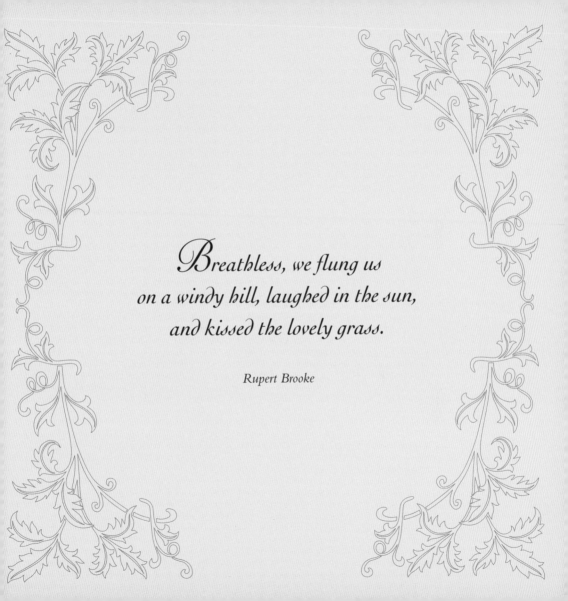

*Breathless, we flung us
on a windy hill, laughed in the sun,
and kissed the lovely grass.*

Rupert Brooke

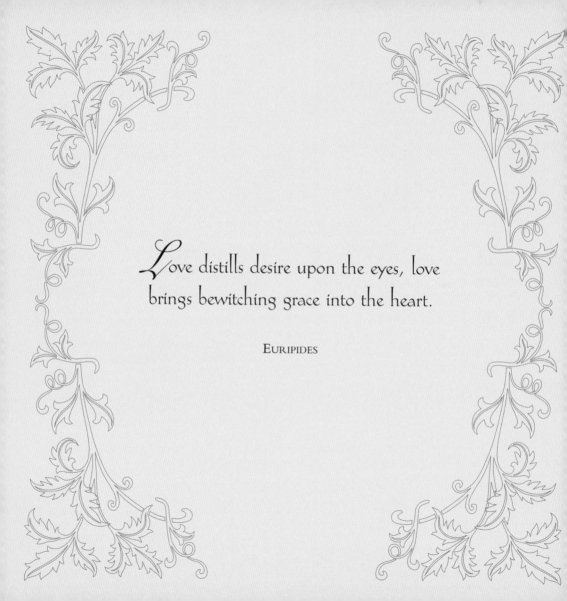

Love distills desire upon the eyes, love
brings bewitching grace into the heart.

EURIPIDES

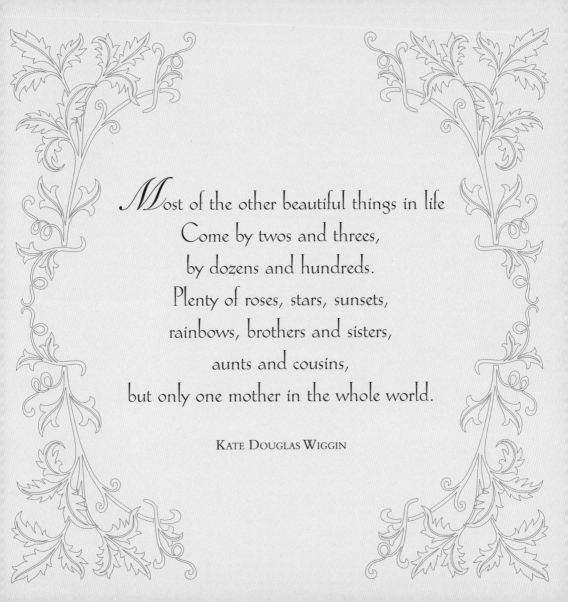

Most of the other beautiful things in life
Come by twos and threes,
by dozens and hundreds.
Plenty of roses, stars, sunsets,
rainbows, brothers and sisters,
aunts and cousins,
but only one mother in the whole world.

KATE DOUGLAS WIGGIN

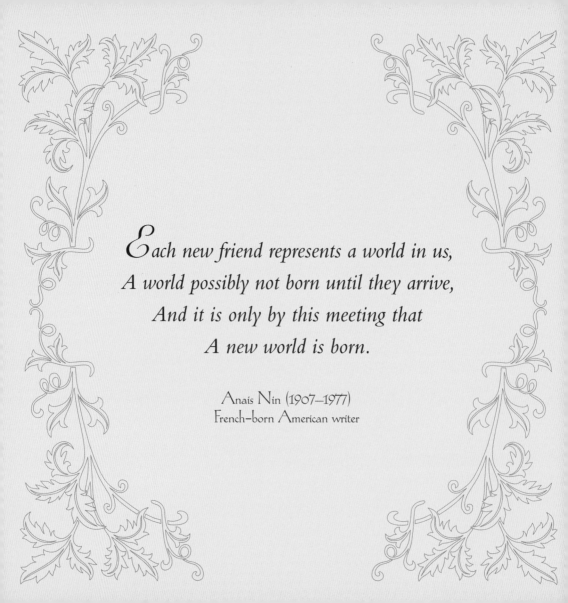

Each new friend represents a world in us,
A world possibly not born until they arrive,
And it is only by this meeting that
A new world is born.

Anaïs Nin (1907–1977)
French–born American writer

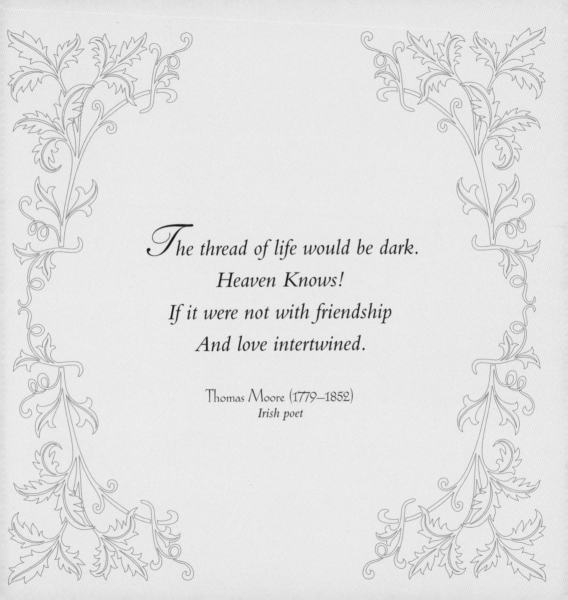

The thread of life would be dark.
Heaven Knows!
If it were not with friendship
And love intertwined.

Thomas Moore (1779–1852)
Irish poet

*T*he best mirror is an old friend.

English proverb

A kiss makes the heart young again
and wipes out the years.

Rupert Brooke

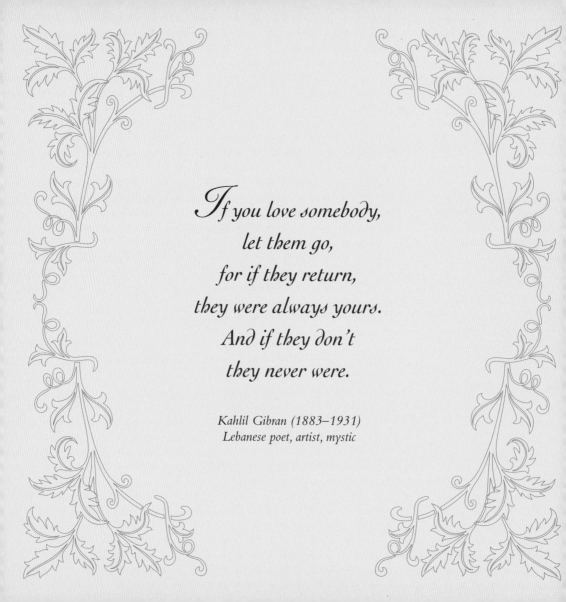

If you love somebody,
let them go,
for if they return,
they were always yours.
And if they don't
they never were.

Kahlil Gibran (1883–1931)
Lebanese poet, artist, mystic

Remember tonight,
for it is the beginning of always.

Dante Alighieri (1265–1321)
Italian epic poet, philosopher

A loving person lives in a loving world.
A hostile person lives in a hostile world:

everyone you meet is your mirror.

KEN KEYES JR.
AMERICAN WRITER

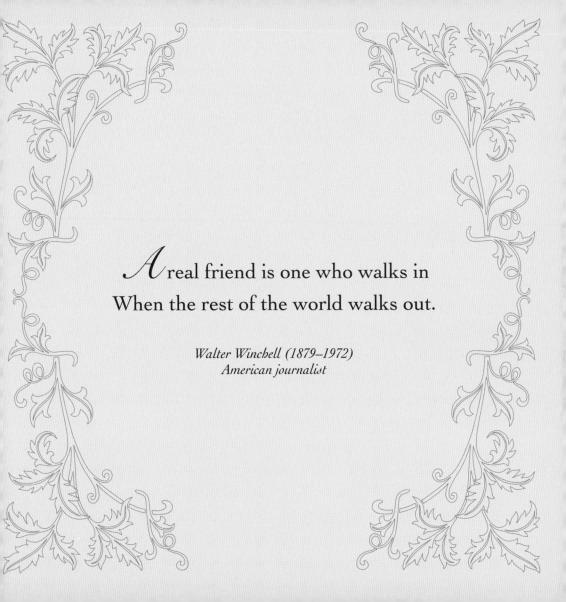

A real friend is one who walks in
When the rest of the world walks out.

Walter Winchell (1879–1972)
American journalist

A hedge between
Keeps friendship green

English proverb

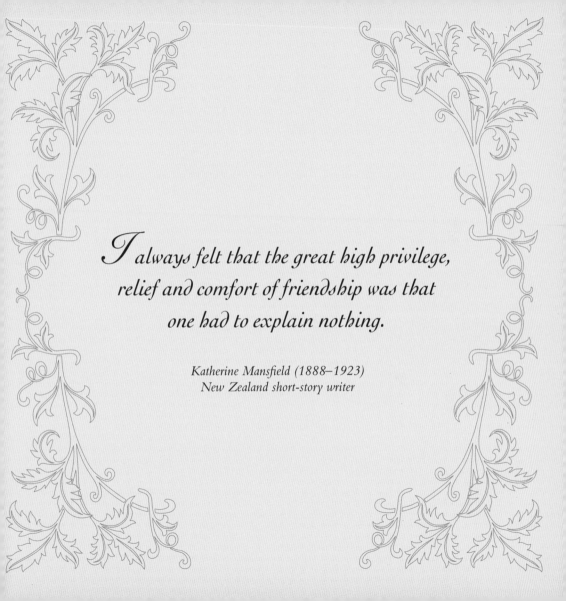

I always felt that the great high privilege,
relief and comfort of friendship was that
one had to explain nothing.

Katherine Mansfield (1888–1923)
New Zealand short-story writer

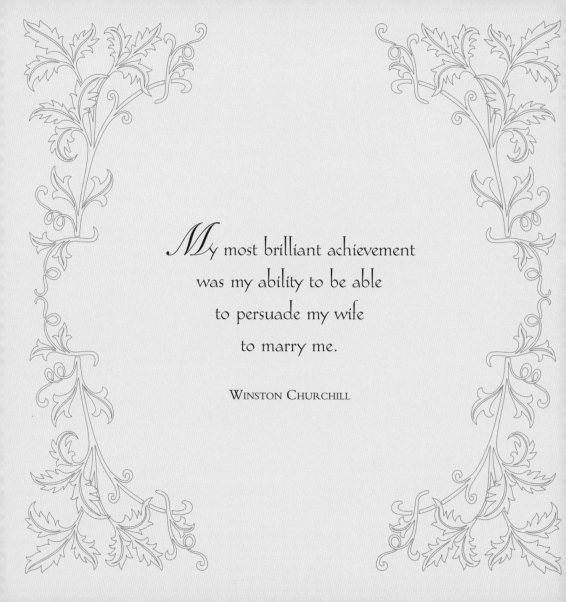

My most brilliant achievement
was my ability to be able
to persuade my wife
to marry me.

WINSTON CHURCHILL

Love is the enchanted dawn of every heart.

ALPHONSE MARIE DE LA MARTINE

I wish I could remember that first day,
First hour, first moment of your meeting me,
If bright or dim the season, it might be
Summer or Winter for aught I can say;
So unrecorded did it slip away,
So blind was I to see and to foresee,
So dull to mark the budding of my tree
That would not blossom for many a May.

Christina Rossetti (1830–1894)
English poet

If all the world and love were young,

and truth in every shepherd's tongue,

these pretty pleasures might me move

to live with thee and be thy love.

Sir Walter Raleigh (1522–1618)
English officer, navigator, historian, poet, courtier

*L*ove bears all things, believes all things,
hopes all things, endures all things.

1 Corinthians 13:7

Here's a sigh
to those who love me,
and a smile
to those who hate;
and whatever sky's above me,
here's a heart
for every fate.

LORD BYRON

It's all I have to bring today,
this, and my heart beside,
this, and my heart, and all the fields,
and all the meadows wide.
Be sure you count, should I forget
someone the sun could tell—
this, and my heart, and all the bees
which in the clover dwell.

Emily Dickinson (1830–1886)
American poet

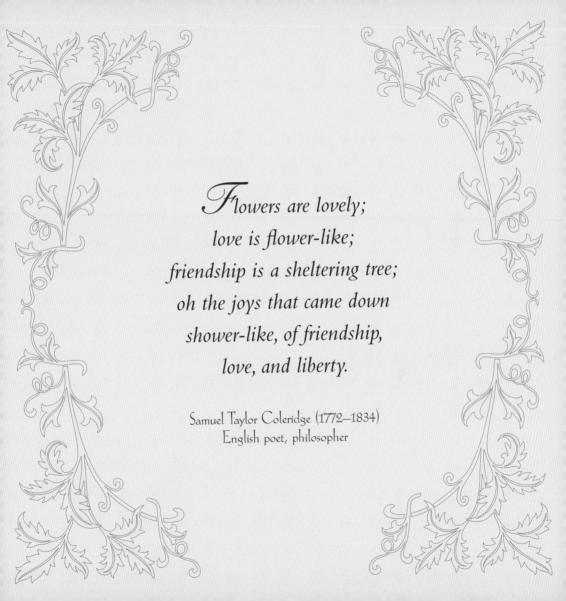

Flowers are lovely;
love is flower-like;
friendship is a sheltering tree;
oh the joys that came down
shower-like, of friendship,
love, and liberty.

Samuel Taylor Coleridge (1772–1834)
English poet, philosopher

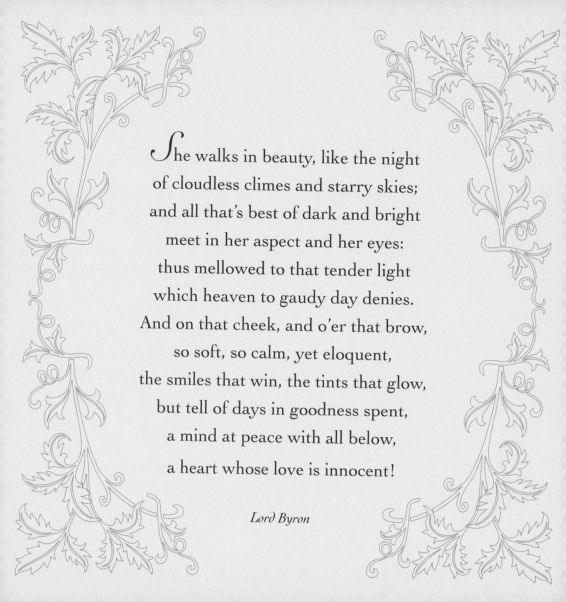

She walks in beauty, like the night
of cloudless climes and starry skies;
and all that's best of dark and bright
meet in her aspect and her eyes:
thus mellowed to that tender light
which heaven to gaudy day denies.
And on that cheek, and o'er that brow,
so soft, so calm, yet eloquent,
the smiles that win, the tints that glow,
but tell of days in goodness spent,
a mind at peace with all below,
a heart whose love is innocent!

Lord Byron

*H*is kiss is sweet, his word is kind,

his love is rich to me;

I could not in a palace find

a truer heart than he.

Thomas Osborne Davis

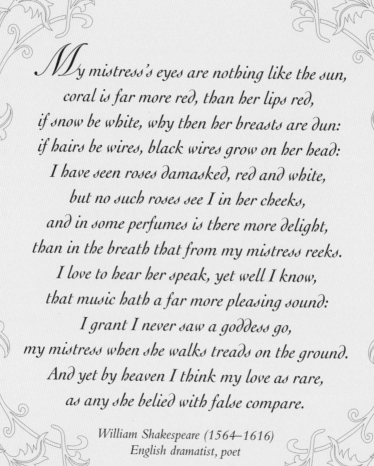

My mistress's eyes are nothing like the sun,
coral is far more red, than her lips red,
if snow be white, why then her breasts are dun:
if hairs be wires, black wires grow on her head:
I have seen roses damasked, red and white,
but no such roses see I in her cheeks,
and in some perfumes is there more delight,
than in the breath that from my mistress reeks.
I love to hear her speak, yet well I know,
that music hath a far more pleasing sound:
I grant I never saw a goddess go,
my mistress when she walks treads on the ground.
And yet by heaven I think my love as rare,
as any she belied with false compare.

William Shakespeare (1564–1616)
English dramatist, poet

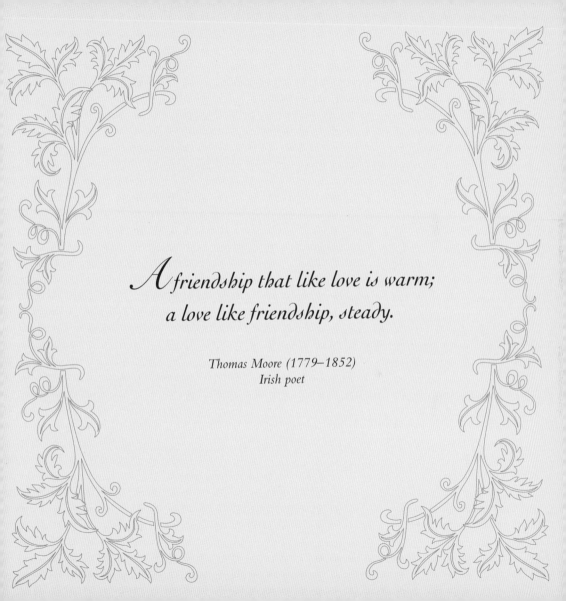

A friendship that like love is warm;
a love like friendship, steady.

Thomas Moore (1779–1852)
Irish poet

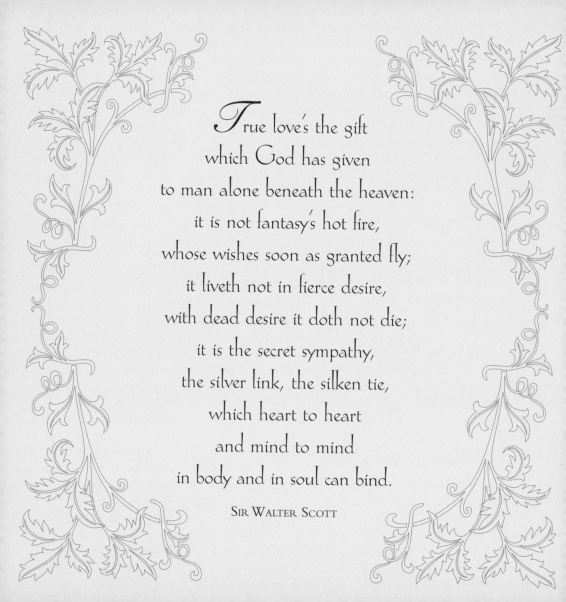

True love's the gift
which God has given
to man alone beneath the heaven:
it is not fantasy's hot fire,
whose wishes soon as granted fly;
it liveth not in fierce desire,
with dead desire it doth not die;
it is the secret sympathy,
the silver link, the silken tie,
which heart to heart
and mind to mind
in body and in soul can bind.

SIR WALTER SCOTT

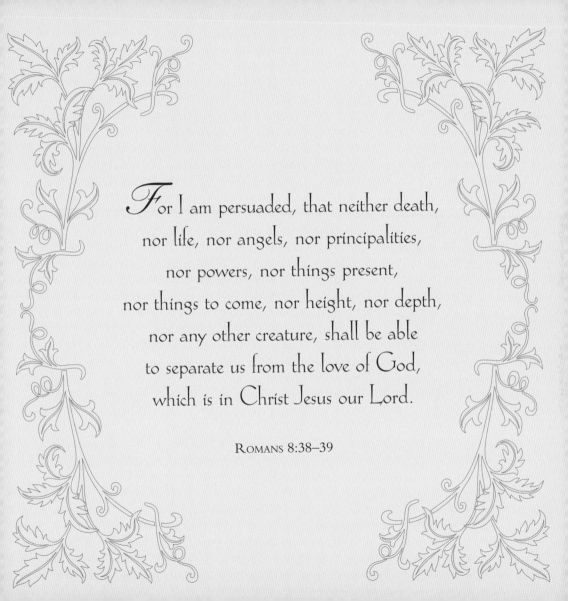

*F*or I am persuaded, that neither death,
nor life, nor angels, nor principalities,
nor powers, nor things present,
nor things to come, nor height, nor depth,
nor any other creature, shall be able
to separate us from the love of God,
which is in Christ Jesus our Lord.

ROMANS 8:38–39

*The road to a friend's
house is never long.*

Danish proverb

Listen to my heart,
can you hear it sing:
Come back to me
and forgive everything.

Moulin Rouge
(the movie)

$\mathcal{I}$t was but a little that I passed from them,
but I found him whom my soul loveth:
I held him, and would not let him go.

Song of Solomon 3: 4

*W*ith true friends, even water
drunk together is sweet enough.

Chinese proverb

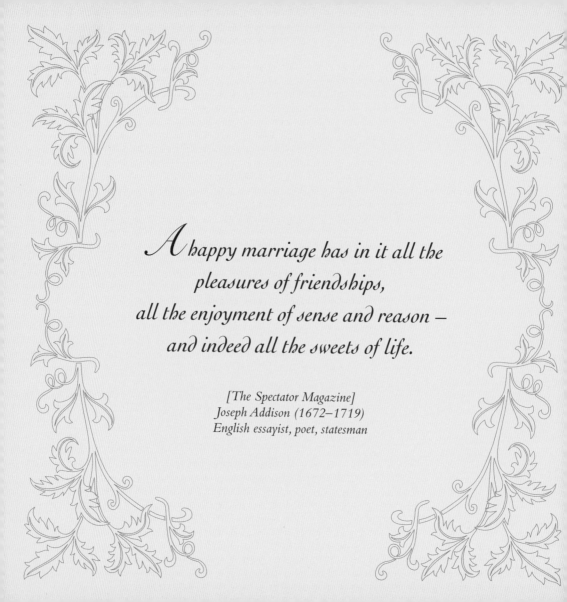

A happy marriage has in it all the
pleasures of friendships,
all the enjoyment of sense and reason —
and indeed all the sweets of life.

[The Spectator Magazine]
Joseph Addison (1672–1719)
English essayist, poet, statesman

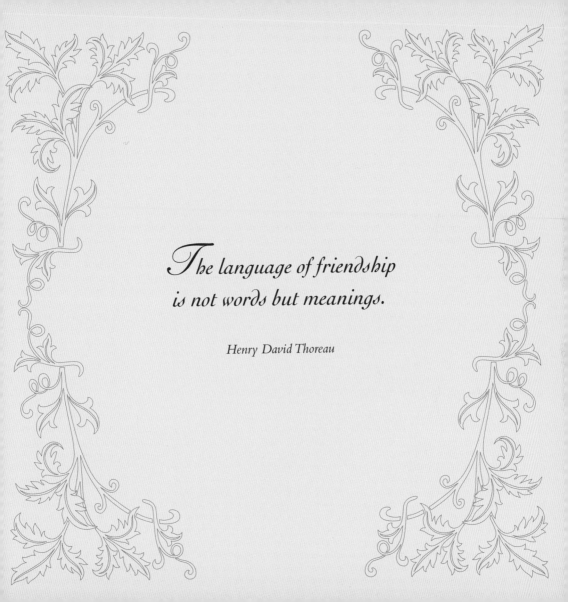

$\mathcal{T}$he language of friendship
is not words but meanings.

Henry David Thoreau

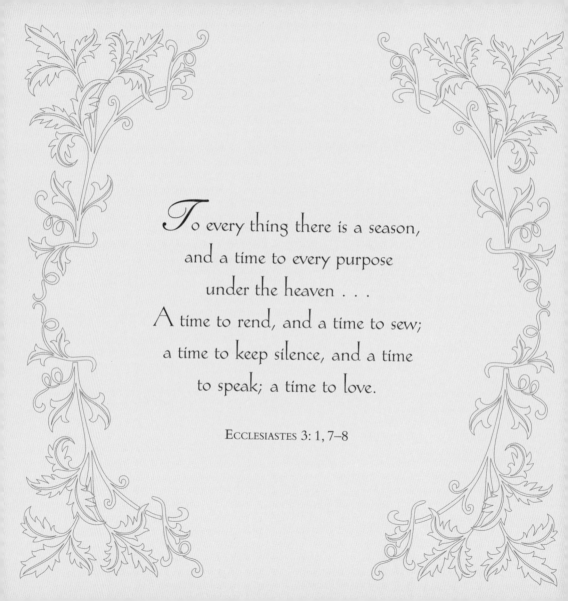

To every thing there is a season,
and a time to every purpose
under the heaven . . .
A time to rend, and a time to sew;
a time to keep silence, and a time
to speak; a time to love.

ECCLESIASTES 3: 1, 7–8

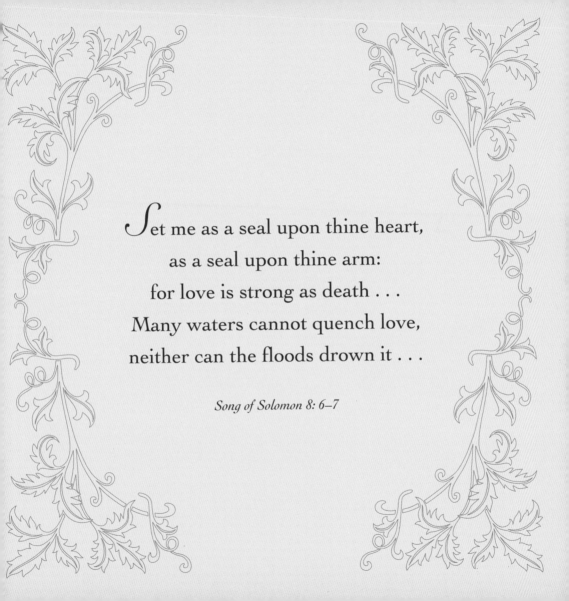

$\mathcal{S}$et me as a seal upon thine heart,

as a seal upon thine arm:

for love is strong as death . . .

Many waters cannot quench love,

neither can the floods drown it . . .

Song of Solomon 8: 6–7

The mother's first kiss
teaches the child love.

Giuseppe Mazzini